MINDFUL COLORING

Illustrated by
Alona Savchuk

iseek

Copyright © 2020 iSeek Ltd.

ISBN: 978-1-64722-314-4

This book was created and produced by iSeek Ltd.
an imprint of Insight Editions
www.insighteditions.com
Insight Editions
PO Box 3088 San Rafael, CA 94912

Designed by Anton Poitier

Printed in China

10 9 8 7 6 5

Let's get coloring.

This book is jam-packed with amazing pictures to color. You can use either felt-tip pens or colored pencils, depending on the effect you like best. There are over 90 pictures in this book, so take a deep breath and take your time.

Pencils or pens?

Choose whether you want to use colored pencils, felt-tip pens, or a combination of both. Lay out all your favorite colors, and pick a set that you like. You can choose different shades of just one or two colors to create a cool effect, or you can use lots of different colors to create a bright and bold picture.

Keep it simple!

You can decide to color only part of the picture, leaving the rest white. This is a really useful way to make something stand out!

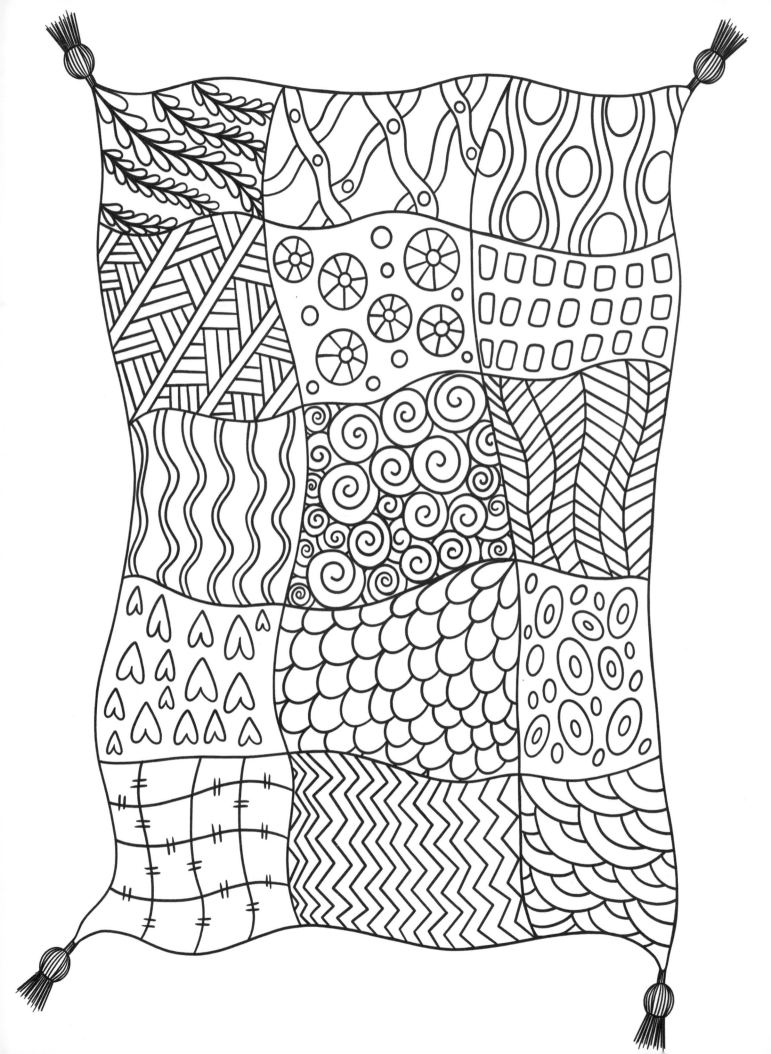

ZOO